I0471693

Hustle How To:

QUICK START GUIDE TO BUILDING A SIDE BUSINESS IF YOU'RE BROKE

Hu$tle
How To:

CONTENTS

ABOUT THE AUTHOR

I CAN RELATE

I grew up just like anyone else. After my parents divorced I moved to the suburbs of Northern Virginia to live with my dad. I grew up an average kid, I was a c student at best and I graduated high school with a 1.8 GPA.

I wanted to go to college but my parents told me that realistically wasn't an option for me, so I enlisted in the US Air Force. After my enlistment I literally couldn't find a job to save my life so I pretty much went to college to survive off my GI Bill BAH and student loans.

My senior year in college at Norfolk State University, I was lucky enough to secure a full-time job with benefits working with the Norfolk Department of Human Services before I graduated.

Unfortunately, I was laid off within a year which was the turning point that set me on my entrepreneurial journey.

IF I CAN DO IT SO CAN YOU

I've struggled a lot since I reached adulthood. I was on my own a lot, and after my military service every day was a battle for survival. I lost my house to foreclosure and had my car repossessed. I struggled to keep a roof over my head, and even had to resort to collecting change on the street to buy a loaf of bread to eat.

I had never experienced the feeling of starvation and it's something ill never forget. It led me to a dark place, I felt alone and depressed and found myself pondering my existence. Feeling like I had nothing to lose I began stealing and selling drugs, and pretty much doing anything to make money. I became obsessed.

Looking
 back now It makes me angry that I thought I had to resort to criminal activity to survive, which is a common belief among poor people.

In hind sight, the reality is I didn't have to do any of those things and I put myself in that situation because I was financially illiterate, and I knew nothing about entrepreneurship. I couldn't find a job but it never occurred to me that creating a job for myself was a viable option.

I thought only rich people start businesses, or I needed good credit and a huge loan to get started, when the reality of it is anyone can start a business and it doesn't take much to get started.

YOU ARE NOT ALONE

I vowed to myself that I would be successful and I would do it the legal way. I left my old life behind and started over with nothing.

I have found success and today I live comfortably. I work for myself, my schedule is as flexible as I want it to be. I travel the world whenever I feel like it and I get to spend time with my son everyday.

I started this project to share my knowledge and help others avoid the mistakes I made. I made it my life's mission to help as many people as I possibly can achieve financial freedom. I know what its like to struggle and be desperate for a way out. You've come to the right place. I am the Get Money Guru and I will guide you every step of the way.

If you ever need a hand or have any questions, feel free to DM me on instagram @getmoneyguru and I will be more than happy to help you out.

All the best,
Jahmaal
@TheMoneyMoses

YOU'RE NOT BROKE

R egardless of your tax bracket we all would like to make more money. Let's face it, money is the core of our modern day society. Unless you are self-sufficient and living off the land you basically need money to live.

If money is so important, why then don't we treat it that way? Most of us don't think about our money until our check is pretty much gone. We spend it on things we don't need and we don't pay it much attention until it's too late.

◆ ◆ ◆

Its all in your head

The average person lives in doors, eats every day and has a monthly household income. If you have these three characteristics you are not broke.

You are probably sitting on money but you just don't see it because your mind has been conditioned to value everything you don't have and nothing you do have. Our society revolves around consumerism, it wouldn't work if everybody was happy with what they already had.

Media, advertisements and social interactions from the time we are children condition us to always want more, bigger, better and faster STUFF. It makes it hard to differentiate between what we need and what we just want.

Either that or you've developed the bad habit of over valuing everything you have. Hoarding and holding on to things over the decades as they sit and collect dust. Either way I get it. You're Broke. So how do we fix it?

* Free Your mind
* Freeup Capital
* Save Your Income
* Invest Your Savings

FREE YOUR MIND & THE REST WILL FOLLOW.

YOU WILL NOT IMPROVE YOUR SITUATION IF YOU DO NOT EXPAND YOUR MIND.

T he reason you haven't reached your goals yet, is because you don't know everything and everyone you need to know yet. Stop waiting for someone to teach you. Teach yourself.

In this day and age many people will proudly say they don't read. Out of the few that do, a lot of them are only reading fantasy and fiction. Lacking education, a degree or a diploma is not holding you back. What's holding you back is your lack of knowledge and in the age of information, we have access to learn pretty much anything we want to.

If you want to know something google it. Read the information from a few different sources in the search results, then go to You-Tube and search. Most of the free information you get will have gaps in it but it is a good start.

After YouTube, BUY A BOOK about it and READ IT!!!. This is the process that is going to get the ball rolling in your favor.

After you've taught yourself as much as you can the next thing to do is to find someone to teach/coach/train you.

Please, I'm begging you! Get in the habit of investing in your own education.

People throw around money like there is no tomorrow on friv-olous things like video games, Netflix, fast food, sneakers, clothes, concerts, beer, cigarettes and weed but become "financially savvy" as soon as they are asked to pay for information or education.

The information is literally at their finger tips but as soon as they are asked to pay for it they are instantly turned off. It's not a scam, it's a business. You want people to spend hours teaching and help-ing you get rich for free? If this sounds like you, we have a lot of work to do.

SAVE YOUR INCOME:

*Give up something for 30 days,
take the money you would have
spent frivolously and invest
it in educating yourself.*

I t could be buying a book (ever thought of buying a textbook for a college class you can't afford?) , taking a class at a local college or trade school or find an online course that interests you from a successful person that you admire.

Here are 3 of my favorites if you don't know where to start:

The $100 Start Up
Rich Dad, Poor Dad
Wealthy Affiliate
Free Up Capital

I had an epiphany one time as I was starving I was so hungry, I hadn't eaten anything in about a day and a half. My bank account was over drafted and I had literally no food in my house.

As I was walking around trying to find a fountain to collect change I started to think about every dollar I had ever had my whole life.

When I was a kid I remember getting money from the tooth fairy, birthdays, Christmas, aunts, uncles and grand-parents. The first thing I did was spend it on candy, ice cream or toys. I was so angry at myself in that moment. I had been getting money my entire life and had nothing to show for it. I imagined how much money I would have if I had saved that money let alone invested it.

I think most people can relate. Especially if you have a job or some source of monthly income. You're actually not broke you are just conditioned to be broke. Take a second to think of what your net worth is. How much money do you earn yearly? Combine that with the total value of all the things you possess.

Now do it again, except this time think of all the things you didn't calculate in the first time. Get rid of those things, they aren't that important. Sell them to free up some money to get yourself started. That broken lawn mower, that old microwave, those books you never read and the ones you already did. How about those video games you don't play anymore. That sneaker collection.... oh sneakers aren't a waste of money? They are worth something right? Sell them you don't need them. What's in your attic? It's time for a yard sale.

Have you ever wondered how immigrants come to your country with nothing and in one generation they are better off than your entire ancestry? From my experience with traveling I'd say it's because their minds are free. They don't care about keeping up with the Jones or the Kardashians.

They probably don't pay for cable because they probably don't care what's on TV. If you don't believe me go online and watch some foreign television and tell me you would pay $100 a month for it.

Do you think they care if anyone sees them with an old android phone? Do you think they care when the new J's come out.

They probably don't understand the fashion trends let alone spend their hard-earned money trying to keep up with them. They left home for an opportunity and they came focused. Every pay check they pay for their necessities and everything else they probably send back to their country or they save it for a later investment.

FREEUP CAPITAL:

Hold a yard sale and/or sell as many items in your house as you can on craigslist, letgo, offerup and eBay.

Cancel at least one (more would be better) of your monthly subscription services for at least 30 days. Save that money! Now that you've completed challenges 1 & 2 you should have some money on hand. If not repeat steps one and two .

Okay so now that you have some extra funds what are we going to do? Save, save and continue saving. If you are not saving money monthly then you are doing something wrong, go back to steps 1 & 2 again lol. We are not saving for a rainy day and we are not saving for the new iPhone or a vacation. We are saving this money so that we can invest it.

But seriously if you are having trouble saving money there are some tools that will help you budget and save your money daily, weekly and monthly.

Here are some of my favorites:

Digit: An app that automates saving for you daily, you won't even notice it's doing it and it won't over draft your account. Click the link and get $5 just for signing up.

Dave: An app that will help you create a budget based on your spending habits and will even front you some money to avoid an overdraft.

Qapital: An app that saves change every time you spend money. You can link with friends and family to save collectively. Click the link to get $5 for signing up.

MoneyLion: Is a great app to get you on track financially. You get a dollar a day just for opening the app and they automate investing for you. They specialize in credit repair also, they will give you a small loan even if your credit is bad and help you boost your credit score when you pay it back. Once the loan is paid off you get the money back that you paid in monthly payments. Click the link to sign up and get a free $20

INVEST YOUR SAVINGS

This is the major key of it all.

I f you want to make more money you are going to have to invest the time and money you already have. Now that you have extra money DO NOT SPEND YOUR SAVINGS UNLESS IT IS AN INVESTMENT.

Investing is a more advanced skill. It's going to take a lot of research and experience to invest your money the right way. By completing steps 1-3 you will start to learn some investments and you will be saving towards those investments.

All investments come with risks so do your research.

Once you start successfully investing your time and money, you will have more free time and your investments will be new sources of income that generate money for you daily, weekly, monthly or yearly.

MAKE MORE MONEY- WHERE TO START

Lean Entrepreneurship – The 100 Dollar Start-Up

Have you ever thought of a great business idea? One that's sure to change your life? The perfect business, but..... there's always a "but".

If I asked you what's stopping you, most likely you would narrow it down to your lack of funds getting in the way of your success as an entrepreneur. If this sounds like you, I would probably tell you its not your lack of funds that's holding you back, its all in your head. Then you probably wouldn't like me very much.

You Don't Need Money to Start a Business!

T he difference between being an entrepreneur and a wantrepreneur is action.

A wantrepreneur dreams of being their own boss, starting a business and changing their life but they never act on their dreams because society has conditioned them to create their own road blocks in their head.

I understand you want your ideas to be perfect, exactly how you dreamed and you maybe don't have the funds yet to make it happen. Don't make the mistake of crossing the finish line before you've even started the race, let alone jumped the first hurdle.

Lean entrepreneurship simply means doing more with less resources to generate income. There are plenty things that you can do today to make some money and get yourself started working on your dreams. Many millionaires started their journey with just 100 dollars or less.

Start Small and Work Your Way Up

D uh!!! Lol. Why is it that we understand this concept as employees but not as entrepreneurs? Many of us started our first job somewhere where we had to ask "Do you want fries with that?" every two minutes. My first job was burger king when I was 15.

I knew this wasn't it for me but I knew I needed to start somewhere. I needed to build experience as well as start earning some money to start. This job at Burger King set me up for Red Lobster which led me to the military, which led me to college and then a state job.

So start a small business today to gain experience as an entrepreneur and to start generating extra income to invest in the big one.

Start a business TODAY! Invest no more than 100 dollars into this start up.

D on't Know Where to Start? Start Here. Knowledge and experience go hand in hand. I can't suggest enough that you buy this book and read it. Spending money on it will be added motivation to actually read it.

I was literally a wantrepreneur for years until I started reading this book. The next day after just reading a few chapters, I started a business that generated an extra $200 a week and took very little time and effort.

Think of a product or service that you can provide and start advertising locally and online.

Accept the challenge and get started today. It's not going to happen on its own you are going to have to make it happen. Make something out of nothing. No more excuses. Let me know how you are doing, I'm here with you every step of the way!

SIDE HUSTLE LIKE A CEO

What's difference between a
side hustle and a business?

T here is no difference, it's all in your head. When you conduct yourself like a business people will treat you that way.

Branding Makes All The Difference

Turn your side hustle into a business by branding it. In most cases you shouldn't need a business license or permit getting started (this is not legal advice do your own research). There is a set amount of money or transactions you can make before you legally need to be licensed.

Create a brand for your side hustle
before you begin to promote
your products and/or services.

P rofessionalism puts people at ease. Have you ever made a transaction on craigslist? It's like one of the most nerve wrecking experiences every time. Have you ever paid more money for something in the store that you knew you could have gotten cheaper on craigslist?

We do this because we like the peace of mind that comes with dealing with a business. You will increase your sales by separating your personal identity from your businesses identity.

$5 Will Make You Look Like A Million Bucks

Fiverr has everything you need to give your side hustle a make over. Order freelance services from other entrepreneurs like graphic design, digital marketing, writing, video animation, business plans and so much more. Most of these services can be bought for just five dollars and delivered within one day.

Give your business a name then visit Fiverr and purchase a logo for your business. Create a Facebook Page for your business as well as an Instagram and twitter account. Upload your newly created logo as your profile picture and start posting your products/services for sale.

Communication Is Key

Now that people know that you have products and services for sale, how will they get in contact with you? Google offers a free call relaying service called Google Voice.

You can get a free phone number that will call up to six different phone numbers when it's called. If you change the desktop site to the Legacy Google Voice version you can change how you phone calls show up on your caller id.

You have the option to see your own google voice number or the callers phone number when you get a call.

Step 1:

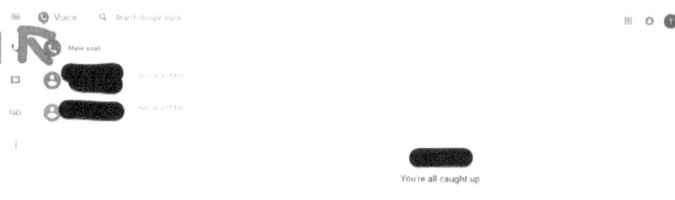

Step 2:

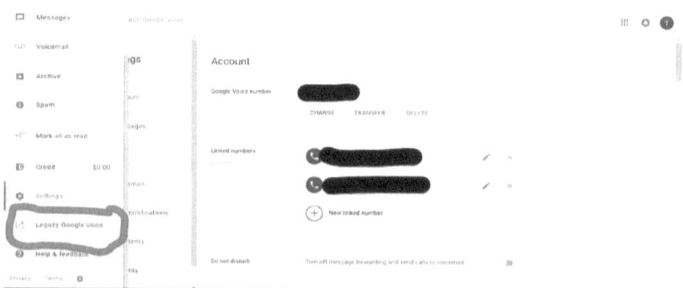

Step 3:

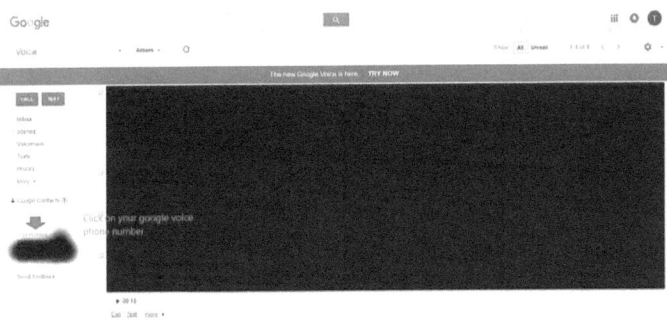

Step 4:

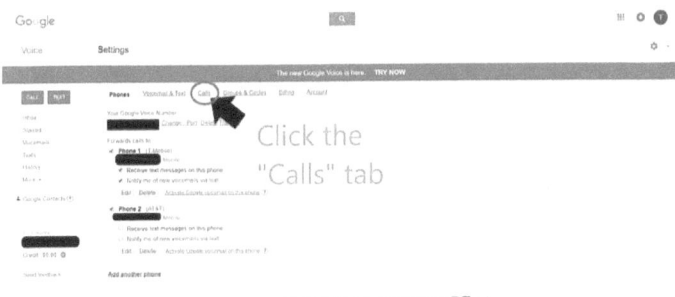

Click the "Calls" tab

Step 5:

I like to change the setting so I see my own google voice number on my caller id whenever someone calls that number. I save my google voice number in my phone's contacts as the name of my business.

Now whenever my phone rings I know whether it's a personal call (in which case I answer "hello?") or a potential customer calling my business (In which case I answer "Thank you for calling *insert business name*, this is Jahmaal speaking").

Fake It Til' You Make It

Now you're ready for business. People are more likely to buy products and services from a business rather than an individual and now you have one.

Look the part, talk the talk and walk the walk. People will treat you according to how professionally you present yourself as an actual business. They will be less likely to ask for handouts or discounts, and more likely to spend higher amounts of money with you.

Don't stop with just a logo, phone number and social media accounts. Get a website, make business cards and once you are profitable with a steady cash flow it's a good idea getting incorporated or an LLC, register with the state and get a business license.

BUSINESS MODEL A

*How to Make Money if You're
Broke – Be a Broker*

Picture this, it's Friday night, you're 10 years old and you are at your best friends house. The hours are rolling by and your mom calls and says she's on her way to pick you up.

You and your friend don't want the party to end and you know at your house your parents will let you stay up all night, eating junk food and playing video games. You ask your mom if your friend can spend the night over and she says yes with no hesitation.

Now for the moment of truth, its time for your best friend to ask their mom if they can stay the night with you. They already know their mom will say no and they are hesitant to ask.

They suggest you should go ask her, "If you ask her, she will say yes". So you ask her and just as planned, she says yes! Congratulations, you just brokered a deal between your best friend and their mom!

Occupation: Middle Man

A broker is someone who arranges transactions between a buyer and a seller for a fee. The art of being a broker is all in the fee. There are brokers in just about every industry of business.

The most important thing about being a broker is making sure you get paid, lets face it you are not necessarily needed in order for the transaction to take place, and both parties would get a better deal if you weren't involved.

The second most important part of being a broker is your sense of self-worth. Without it you will just end up doing favors for people and hoping they leave you a tip. Don't let anyone belittle your role as a broker. You did the work, you deserve to get paid because without you the buyer and seller probably would have never made the connection in the first place.

Broker Fee: Make Sure You Get Paid

One of the first businesses I started after reading the $100 Dollar Start-up was a brokerage business.

I was living in Norfolk, VA off of Ingleside Dr and I noticed a homeless man who lived in one of the vacant houses. He had a lawnmower and he would always ask me if he could cut my grass. He would only charge me $5 – $10 for one yard.

I noticed most of the neighbors didn't want to talk to him and wouldn't open their door when he would come knock. I thought to myself this guy does good work but nobody is going to give him a chance because of his presentation. He wasn't very well-spoken and he didn't have presentable clothes.

I had a conversation with him about it but I knew he would be a lot better off if I were to help him out. I went to Fiverr.com and purchased a logo for $5 and created some business cards.

I put on a suit and went door to door selling lawn care services from a veteran owned business with rates cheaper than any competitors. I was charging $20 a yard out of which I kept $10 and gave the homeless man his fee of $10.

Within the first week I had secured 12 new customers. That's $120 for each of us. He was grateful to have so many new customers and I had built a system of residual income that was generating money for me every other week.

We Aren't in the Business of Doing Favors: You Deserve to Get Paid

I began scaling the business by branching out to other neighborhoods and finding other workers who were offering lawn care services freelance on craigslist.

I found that lawn care services were commonly being offered by foreign immigrants, ex convicts and just less fortunate people in general. A lot of them lacked communication skills and it was immediately evident when reading their ads. Many of them came from Spanish speaking countries (I studied Spanish in HS, college and abroad) or just lacked business savvy.

Socially there is a stigma commonly associated with this demographic of people, which is what made me so valuable to them as a broker and their work ethic and skills are what made them valuable to me as a seller.

Whatever their fee was I just added $10- $20 at the most and $5 at the least. All I had to do was put on my suit and go make deals happen.

> *"Hello, my name is Jahmaal. I'm with Bombs Away Landscaping. We are a veteran owned business just opening in the local area. I just wanted to let you know about the specials we have going on this summer."*

This is how you side hustle like a CEO. I ended up making an extra $875 a month until I moved to New Jersey that fall.

I never cut one blade of grass.

Being a Broker is a Mindset

 **Y**ou can do the same thing I did in your local area. You can also do this online without ever leaving your home.

I will dig deeper into different ways to be the middle man in later publications, I just wanted to get you familiar with the concept and get your gears turning.

Do you know of anyone who offers any goods or services for sale? It can be an individual or a business. Add a little onto the price then find a buyer or customer.

If you can't find someone to pay what you are asking, contact the seller and see if you can talk their price down and you keep the difference. It's that simple.

Contact me on instagram @getmoneyguru and let me know of any different opportunities you can think of to make money as a broker in your area.

BUSINESS MODEL B

Dropshipping 101 – The
Art of Finesse

I f you've ever googled "how to make money online", then you've probably heard of drop shipping.

If not, then this article is going to blow your mind.

Drop shipping is one of the best methods to make money online if you have absolutely no money or experience. Why? Because you can get started with no money or experience.

What is drop shipping?

D rop shipping just means you are selling someone else's products online that you don't own. Once you make the online sale, you purchase the product online and have it shipped directly to your customer.

You make a profit from this method by simply selling it for more than the price you will have to pay for the item. You can also increase your profit margins with your shipping methods.

Basically if you can copy & paste you can make money online!

For example if you have an amazon prime account you get free 2-day shipping. Without prime, 2-day shipping may cost someone $40-60 on a purse.

You can copy and paste the pictures from Amazon into an eBay listing and offer 2-day shipping for $20.

So a customer is more likely to purchase the purse from you on eBay and pay you $20 for 2-day shipping if you've listed for the same price that it is on Amazon.

When the customer pays you, you go on amazon and purchase the purse, then in the shipping section you enter the customers shipping information, select a gift receipt and have the purse shipped to the customer as a gift via prime 2-day shipping.

Jahmaal Benford

Keep in mind you have amazon prime so it costs you nothing to ship the purse. Congratulations, you just made $20 and all you did was copy & paste.

I started a drop shipping business over the summer. It has been a great new source of income and has been growing steadily.

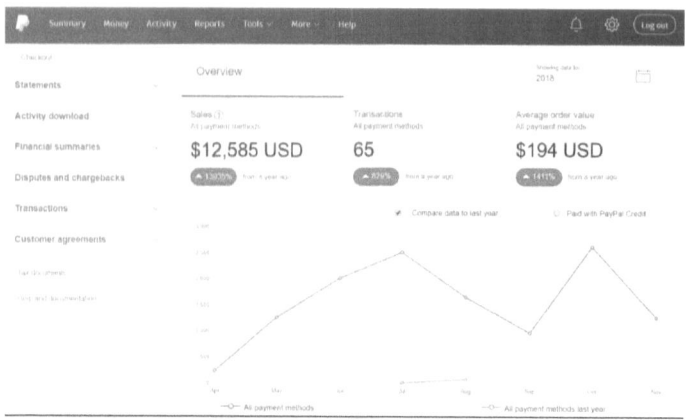

This is not scamming it's the art of the deal!

I ve had people who don't know anything about business say drop shipping is a scam... I say working a 9-5 your whole life until you die is a scam but that's just me....

Do your research, drop shipping is legitimate business, there is a whole industry behind it and people are making millions.

The basic principle of any commerce is you have to sell a product for more than it costs you.

No matter if you opened a brick and mortar store front or a shopify store.

If you found a purse maker who was selling purses for $5 and you sold them for $20 you would feel like a big shot.

It's the same with drop shipping except you are mitigating the risk of buying inventory and possibly not being able to sell the products.

You can play with your profit margins by bumping the price and/or the shipping costs. Drop shipping is the future of e-commerce (it's actually a pretty old method).

Start Drop shipping today!
Get in the game!

I n my opinion the 3 best platforms to start your drop shipping business on are Amazon Prime, eBay & Shopify.

Create an account on all three platforms and get started today.

Create a shopify store website as your main hub for your business.

Link your eBay account to your shopify store to increase profits.

Source products from amazon, aliexpress, etsy or anywhere really

and sell them on eBay and shopify.
It's that simple…

BUSINESS MODEL C

No Product, No Service, No problem.

The easiest way to make money online in my opion is affiliate marketing. It's really similar to the first two business models I suggested because you dont need to create your own products or services, and with this option you dont even need to create your own brand. You're just another middle man working behind the scenes.

Large companies will simply pay you comissions to market their products and services online. They provide you with a unique link id that you send to others. When they click the link and sign up or purchase the company sends you a commission.

The possibilities are endless.

Just about every website you can think of probably has an affiliate program. One of the largest ones is Amazon Associates (google it).

Thats right you can link people to products on Amazon that have nothing to do with you and when the person makes a purchase you get a comission from Amazon.

This process becomes really lucrative once you start building a solid email list of buyers and/or learn how to run facebook and google sponsored ads.

Most likely most of the ads you've seen in your Facebook or Instagram feed arent actually coming from the company being advertised. When you see an ad on your social media its probably coming from someone like myself, maybe a digital nomad or a parent who works from home part-time.

All you need to get started
is an affiliate account and an
internet connection.

S tart promoting some of your favorite products or subscription services today. Just do a quick google search of the company name and add the word "affiliate" behind it.

Sign up for their affiliate account to get your personalized affiliate tracking link.

Send the link to anyone you think would be interested in the product. Post the link in facebook groups and blogs. Post the link in your instagram bio or create a website or youtube channel where you review products and online subscription services. Embed your custom links and move on to the next.

Eventually you will have affiliate links all over the internet driving traffic to the products and services you are promoting.

Set it and forget it.

O nce your links are posted you can leave them alone for the most part. You will start to earn passive residual income for as long as the links stay posted and people click them.

BONUS: AN EASY AFFILIATE PROGRAM TO PROMOTE OR USE TO CUT DOWN YOUR MONTHLY BILLS AND SAVE MONEY

There's one thing that we all love and that's Entertainment.

R egardless of genre most people have a favorite show or movies that they must see but nobody wants to overpay for the entertainment we all love. The growing trend in the entertainment industry is cutting cable.

We all know someone who traded their cable/satellite for a fire stick and Netflix or Hulu subscription. This solution works to some extent but Netflix only shows a limited range of series and movies. Its the same with Hulu & Amazon, which can be pricey if you actually want to enjoy the programs live, like sporting events.

Now there is an all in one solution
that only requires a Wifi connection.

Y ou can now enjoy all of your favorite channels live like HBO, ShowTime, Cinemax, and never miss another live sporting event whether its Pay-Per view or your local NBA/NFL/NHL/MLB team or any game in the country.

You can now get an all inclusive television package for just $25/ m on average ! That's right just $25 per month, with no contracts. You just renew each month you want the service.

Even better you can get paid each month by referring your friends, family or anyone who will listen. For each person you refer you will receive a commission of each purchase month after month reoccurring.

Iv'e been enjoying my IPTV service for months saved thousands of dollars by canceling my $250 direct TV service and after referring my family and friends not only am I getting my service for free, I'm actually making monthly income by helping everyone else save money.

Check Out different IPTV service providers to find one that you like and get started.

Jahmaal Benford

Feel free to DM me on instagram @getmoneyguru if you have any questions or want to just say hi and let me know how much you love your new TV subscription.

Let's Make Some Money,

Jahmaal Benford

CONCLUSION

This is just the beginning.

This concludes my quick start guide. This was by no means intended to be the last book you ever read. Sure you should be ready to get started after reading this book but you are going to need a lot more in depth training if you are going to change your life.

I urge you to do further reasearch into the topics and business models I just discussed.

Pick one of the business models you liked the most and refer back to chapter 2.

Do some google searches and read more on that topic. Then go to youtube.

Then buy a book specific to that business model that is an indepth guide.

Then choose and pay for an online coach & course to really take you to the next level.

Contact me on Instagram @getmoneyguru if you would like some suggestions, tips or further guidance on the subject.

www.ingramcontent.com/pod-product-compliance
Lightning Source LLC
Chambersburg PA
CBHW021939170526
45157CB00005B/2356

* 9 7 8 1 0 9 7 3 6 3 8 4 1 *